Prélude à "L'après-midi d'un faune"

•

Trois Nocturnes

Claude Debussy

DOVER PUBLICATIONS, INC.
Mineola, New York

CONTENTS

Prélude à "L'après-midi d'un faune" (1892–4). . . 1
[Prelude to "The afternoon of a faun," inspired
by the poem of the same name by Stéphane Mallarmé]

Nocturnes (1897–9). 32

I. Nuages [Clouds] 32

II. Fêtes [Festivals] 49

III. Sirènes [Sirens] 102

Copyright

Bibliographical Note

This Dover edition, first published in 1999, is a new compilation of two works originally published in early authoritative editions. The *Prélude* was originally published in 1895; the *Nocturnes,* in 1900.

International Standard Book Number: 0-486-40865-5

Manufactured in the United States of America
Dover Publications, Inc., 31 East 2nd Street, Mineola, N.Y. 11501

Prélude à "L'après-midi d'un faune"

[Prelude to "The afternoon of a faun"]

5

HAUTB.

CL.

1°

CORS

3°

Artemis

1re HARPE

glissando

2e HARPE

(sourdine)

Div.

(sourdine)

Div.

(sourdine)

Div. (sourdine)

11
1
1re FL.
SOLO
p
HAUTB.
p
expressif
CL.
pp
pp
Bons
1o
p
1o
p
CORS
3o
p
1
Div.
(sur la touche)
pp
(sur la touche)
pp
(sur la touche)
pp
à 2
pp

idea starts in winds + goes to strings → contrast
rationality vs irrationality (sensuality)
man goat/animal ⇒ faun
winds strings

21
2
1re FL.
SOLO
légèrement et expressif
p
2e
pp
CORS
4e
pp
8
1re HARPE
pp
2e HARPE
pp
2
pp
pp
pp
Div.
pizz.
pp

23
1re FL.
CL.
Bons
1er COR
1re HARPE
2e HARPE
Unis
pizz.
Unis.
pp
p
1°

poem - two pipes

26

p

FL.

2

CL.

Bons

CORS

2e et 4e

pp

1re HARPE

2e HARPE p

Div.
arco

Div.

arco

arco

28
FL.
Bons
Div.
Unis
arco
Unis
Div.
dim.
Div.
30
FL.
CL.
1°
sourdines
CORS
sourdines
1re HARPE
3
ôtez vite les sourdines
ôtez vite les sourdines
ôtez vite les sourdines
pizz.
Augmentation
B
Disappearence

32
1re FL.
whole tone
mf
CL.
whole tone
mf
p
Bons
1o
p
sf
p
CORS
p
sf
p
1re HARPE
p
p
p
pizz.
sfz
pizz.
arco
sfz
p
pizz.
arco
sfz
p
p
pizz.
arco
sfz
pp
p
Div.
p

35
1re FL.
4
En animant
HAUTB.
1° SOLO
doux et expressif
CL.
Bons
1°
CORS
1re HARPE
4
En animant
pizz.
Div.
arco
pizz
pizz.
Unis

38
HAUTB.
(à 2)
cre - - scen - - do mf
COR ANGL.
cre - - scen - - do mf
CL.
1°
cresc.
(2)
Bons.
cresc.
mf
1. 2.
cresc.
CORS
3. 4.
3°
p
mf
arco
cresc
mf
cre - - scen - do mf
cre - - scen - - do mf
arco
cre - - scen - - do mf
Div.
p
arco
mf

dialogue
poem: tuning up my A
42
5
Toujours en animant
1°
FL.
2° 3°
cresc.
HAUTB
2°
COR ANGL.
CL.
Changez en Sib
à 2
B^ons
CORS
Div.
Unis

45
FL.
HAUTB.
COR ANGL.
CL.
B^ons
CORS
Div.
mf
f
f très en dehors
f (en dehors)
3° (en dehors)
1°
più f
dim.

49
retenu
6
1er mouvt
FL.
dim.
ppp
HAUTB.
COR ANGL.
CL.
Solo
p doux et expressif
Bons
CORS
1r. HARPE
2e. HARPE
retenu
Div.
6
1er mouvt
dim.
pizz.

54
A section
Même mouvt et très soutenu
p expressif et très soutenu
mf
FL.
HAUTB.
p expressif et très soutenu
mf
COR. ANGL.
p expressif et très soutenu
mf
CL.
p expressif et très soutenu
mf
BONS
pp
pp
p
CORS
(3. 4.)
pp
pp
Même mouvt et très soutenu
p
pp
pp
pp
arco
pp
pp
pp
pp
Ab7
Db
Dissappearance

59
7
cre
scen
do
FL.
2° et 3°
HAUTB.
à 2
COR ANGL.
CL.
Bons
1°
cresc
1.2.
CORS
3.4.
4°
7
cresc.
Unis
Unis
Div.
Unis

A
63
FL.
HAUTB.
COR ANGL.
CL.
Bons
à 2
CORS
1re HARPE
2e HARPE
Unis très expressif et très soutenu
pp subito
cre
Div.

66
FL.
HAUTB.
a 2
COR ANGL.
CL.
Bons
CORS
1re HARPE
2e HARPE
scen - - - do
cre - - scen - - do molto
mp

69
B'
FL.
HAUTB.
COR ANGL.
CL.
Bons
à 2
CORS
3e
4e
1re HARPE
2e HARPE
mf
f
ff

72
A
Fl.
Cl.
1°
1
p très doux
B.ons
Cors
p espressif et doux
3°
1re Harpe
sfz
1er V.on solo
p doux et expressif
Div.
sourdines
sourdines
sourdines
sourdines

76
HAUTB.
CL.
CORS
Von SOLO
pp très doux
ppp
più p
79
1re FL.
8 Mouvt du Début
doux et expressif
1re HARPE
(1rs Vns)
Div.

82
1re FL.
Un peu plus animé
pp
HAUTB.
p
sf
CL.
pp
Bons
pp
1.2.
sourdines
CORS
3.4.
sourdines
3°
1re HARPE
préparez le ton de Mib
Un peu plus animé
pizz.
pizz.
pizz.
pizz.

84
1
FL.
2.3.
HAUTB.
p
sfz
pp
COR ANGL.
CL.
Bons
1°
CORS
sur la touche
arco
pizz
Div.

P4 not T1

86

HAUTB. 9 1er mouvt

doux et expressif

p

CORS

1re HARPE *pp*

2e HARPE accordez sur SI♯-DO♮, RÉ♯-MI♭, FA♯-SOL♭, LA♯-SI♭

9

1er mouvt

pos. nat.

pos. nat.

Div.

pos. nat.

Unis.

Div.

Div.

89
dans le mouvt plus animé
1.
FL.
2. 3.
HAUTB.
COR ANGL.
sfz
CL.
Changez en La
Bous
CORS
3o
1re HARPE
2e HARPE
glissando
dans le mouvt plus animé
pizz.
pizz.
pizz.
pizz.

91
1.
FL.
2. 3.
p
HAUTB.
p
COR ANGL.
p
sf
mf
CL.
pp
p
3
Bons
pp
1o cuivré
CORS
pp
glissando
2e HARPE
arco
Div.
arco
pizz.
arco
Unis.
arco
pizz.
arco
Unis.
pp

93
retenu
10 Dans le 1er mouvt avec plus de langueur
Fl.
p expressif et doux
2°
p
Cor Angl.
mf
Cl.
pp
pp
1° bouché
naturel
pp
Cors
3° et 4°
pp
Cymb. antiques
pp
10
Deux 1rs Vns
sans sourdines
pp très doux et expressif
retenu
pp
sur la touche
pp
1rs Vns Divisés
sur la touche
pp
sur la touche
pp
2ds Vns Divisés
sur la touche
pp
sur la touche
pp
Altos Divisés
sur la touche
pp
Div.
sur la touche
pp

96
FL.
HAUTB. 1°
CL.
à 2
Bons
1°
1r sourdine
CORS
3e et 4e
CYMB. ANT.
1 Vlle SOLO

99
P4
FL.
HAUTB.
CL.
Bons
CORS
sourdine
2o
CYMB. ANT.
1re HARPE
pos. nat.
pos. nat.
pos. nat.
pos. nat.
pos. nat.
pos. nat.
1 Vlle SOLO

102
11
Retenu
(a tempo)
Très retenu
1re Fl.
HAUTB.
SOLO
COR ANGL.
CL.
Bons
CORS
Retenu
(a tempo)

reconciliation?
106
12
Très lent et très retenu jusqu'à la fin
FL.
2. 3.
HAUTB.
1. 2.
(sourdines)
CORS
3. 4.
(sourdines)
CYMB. ANT.
1re et 2e HARPES
12
Très lent et très retenu jusqu'à la fin
Unis
Div.
pizz.
pizz.

Nocturnes

I. Nuages

[Clouds]

5
FL.
1
COR ANG.
expressif
3
p
pp
CL.
1er et 2e Bons
CORS
TIMB.
tr
ppp
pppp
8
Div. en 6

11
TIMB.
1ers vons
à 3
pp
à 2
2ds vons
ALTOS
pizz.
16
COR ANG.
très expressif
(un peu en dehors)
velles
Div.

22
COR ANG.
3
p
1o
p
CORS
3o
p
2ds vons
ALTOS
pp
velles
pp
pp

27
COR ANG.
3
CORS
3

32
HAUTB.
1o
p
CL.
Bons
CORS
pp

37
HAUTB.
à 2
p
cre - scen - do
CL.
Bons
à 4

42
4
HAUTB
COR ANG
CL
BONS
1°
CORS
3°
4
pizz.
pizz.
pizz.
pizz.
Div.

46
COR ANG.
5
1er COR
sourdines
p
5
pizz.
pizz.
arco
pizz.
arco
pp

50
COR ANG
1er et 2e Bons
pp
1er COR
p
più p
pp
54
HAUTB.
COR ANG
6
p expressif
pp
ALTO SOLO
sans sourdines
p expressif
ppp

59

HAUTB.

pp

CL.

pp

pp

BONS

pp

pp

pp

pp

pp

ALTO SOLO

più p

pp

pp

pp

pp

pp

pp

pp

pp

64
7 Un peu animé
1re FL.
1o
très expressif
CL.
pp
1er et 2e Bons
pp
pp
HARPE
(Sol♭, Ré♭, La♭, Mi♭, Si♭)
7 Un peu animé
pp
pp
pp
pp
pp
pp
pp
pp
pp

69
1re Fl.
pp
Cl.
1o sourdines
pp
pp
pp
Cors
3o sourdines
pp
Harpe
1 Von SOLO (sans sourdines)
p très expressif et très soutenu
p
pp
pp
pp
pp
pp
Alto SOLO
pp
pp
très expressif et très soutenu
pp
pp
pp
pp
Velle SOLO
sans sourdines
très expressif et très soutenu
pp
pp
pp
pp
pp
pp
pizz.
pp
arco

74
8
1re Fl.
Cl.
1er et 2e Bons
Cors
1o
3o
Harpe
8
Von solo
Alto solo
Velle solo
p
pp
ppp

79

1re FL.

1° tempo

più **p** *molto dim.*

pp

COR ANG.

3

sfz > **p**

p >

3

p < <

CL.

sfz > **p** >

pp

p

sfz > **p** >

pp

p

1er et 2e Bons

1°

sf > **p** >

pp

CORS

> **p**

più **p** > **pp**

3°

> **p**

più **p** > **pp**

HARPE

0

1° tempo

sur la touche

pp

sur la touche

pp

sur la touche

pp

sur la touche

pp

85
HAUTB.
1°
p
più p pp
9
COR ANG.
p molto dim.
CL.
p
più p pp
CORS
3°
p
più p pp
TIMB.
tr
ppp
9
pp
pp
pp
pp
pp
pp
à 4
sur la touche
pp

91
COR ANG.
Plus lent
10
pp
1er et 2e Bons
pp
1o
pp
TIMB.
tr
ppp
pp
pp
pp
à 8
pp
pp
à 4
ppp
97
Encore plus lent
1re FL.
SOLO
CORS
Sourdines
pp
ppp
TIMB.
tr
pp
pp
pizz.
pp
ppp
pizz.
pp
pizz.
pp
pizz.
pp
pizz.
pp
pizz.
pp
ppp
più pp
pizz.
pp
ppp
pizz.
pp
ppp
pizz.
pizz.
pp
ppp

II. Fêtes

[Festivals]

4
COR ANG.
CL.
1er et 2e Bons
CORS
1re et 2e TROMP.

8

1re et 2e FL.
à 2
p

HAUTB.
à 2
p

COR ANG.
ff

CL.
ff

1er et 2e Bons
ff

ff

CORS
ff

1re et 2e TROMP.

ff

ff

Div.
pp
pp

Div.
pp
pp

Div.
pp

12
1re et 2e FL.
HAUTB.
CL.
1er et 2e Bons
1
p
Div.
Unis.
Unis.
16
1re et 2e FL.
HAUTB.
COR ANG.
CL.
1er et 2e Bons
3e et 4e CORS
(Bouché)
sfz
à 2
cre - scen -
cresc.
Div.
Unis.

20

1re et 2e FL.

retenu

-scen - - - - - do

HAUTB.

-scen - - - - - do

COR ANG.

-scen - - - - - do

CL.

-scen - - - - - do

à 2

-do

f

à 2

ff

BONS

ff

1er et 2e CORS

(cuivrez)

f

ff

TROMP.

ff

ff

TROMB.

TIMB.

tr

fff

retenu

-scen - - - - - do

-scen - - - - - do

-scen - - - - - do

-scen - - - - - do

Unis.

-scen - - - - - do

ff

24
COR ANG.
A tempo
2
Un peu plus animé
CL.
Changez en LA
Bons
TROMP.
TROMB.
1re HARPE
(glissando)
2e HARPE
(glissando)
TIMB.
CYMB.
A tempo
2
Un peu plus animé
pizz.
pizz.
pizz.
pizz.

28

1re et 2e FL.

HAUTB.

COR ANG.

CL.

Bons

CORS

TIMB.

Div. arco

Div. arco

Div. arco

Div. arco

32

1res et 2e FL.

HAUTB.

COR ANG.

CL.

Bons

3e et 4e CORS

TIMB.

pizz.

pizz.

pizz.

35
1re et 2e FL.
3
HAUTB.
à 2
COR ANG.
CL.
à 2
très marqué
Bons
f très marqué
CORS
f très marqué
TIMB.
3
arco
mf
arco
mf
arco
mf
mf

40

COR ANG.

p

CL.

p

p

Bons

p

CORS

p

p

Div.

pp

p *expressif*

44
1re et 2e FL.
HAUTB.
à 2
COR ANG.
CL.
Bons
3e COR
Div. pizz.
Div.
pizz.

48

FL.
HAUTB.
CL.
1er et 2e Bons
CORS
4o
Div.
arco
Div.
arco
Div.
arco
dim.
dim.

53
HAUTB.
4
1o
p
3e et 4e CORS
p
pp très léger
pp très léger
pizz.
pp
pizz.
pp

57
HAUTB.
1er et 2e Bons
1o
p
Div.
pp
pp
p
pp

61
1re et 2e FL.
p
HAUTB.
1o
p
CL.
1o
p
pp
Bons
pp
1re et 2e TROMP.
4
p mais un peu en dehors
p
Div.
p

66
1re et 2e FL.
cre
scen
do
mf sempre cresc.
HAUTB.
2o
cre
scen
do
mf sempre cresc.
COR ANG.
mf
CL.
mf sempre cresc.
Bons
mf sempre cresc.
3e et 4e CORS
mf sempre cresc.
1re et 2e TROMP.
5
Div.
cre
scen
do
mf
Unis.
arco

71
1re et 2e FL.
molto cresc.
HAUTB.
molto cresc.
COR ANG.
molto cresc.
CL.
molto cresc.
molto cresc.
Bons
molto cresc.
3e et 4e CORS
molto cresc.
molto cresc.
molto cresc.
molto cresc.
molto cresc.

76
FL.
HAUTB.
à 2
COR ANG.
CL.
à 2
BONS
à 2
CORS
TIMB.
Unis.
Unis.
Div.

81
6
FL.
HAUTB.
COR ANG.
CL.
à 2
à 2
p
p
Bons
CORS
p
p
TIMB.
pp
6
Div. par 3.
pp
Div. par 3.
pp
Div.
pp
pp
pizz.
pp

86
1re et 2e FL.
7
pp
HAUTB. à 2
p expressif (un peu en dehors)
COR ANG.
p expressif (un peu en dehors)
CL.
à 2
p
1er et 2e Bons
à 2
p
2o
p
1o
CORS
4o
p
3o
p
TIMB.
pp
7
pp
pp
pp
pp
Unis.
tr
pp
pp
Div.
p
pizz.
pp

91
COR ANG.
p expressif e cresc.
CL.
p
p expressif e cresc.
p
p
Bons
p
(Bouchez et cuivrez)
p
CORS
(Bouchez et cuivrez)
p
TIMB.
p cresc.
p cresc.
tr
tr
p cresc.
arco
p cresc.
(arco)
p cresc.

96
8
1re et 2e FL.
HAUTB.
1o
COR ANG.
CL.
Bons
CORS
TIMB.
pizz.
Div.
Unis
tr
sfz
f

101
1re et 2e FL.
p cresc.
HAUTB.
p cresc.
COR ANG.
p cresc.
CL.
p cresc.
2o
p cresc.
sf
Bons
p cresc.
sfz
1o
p cresc.
sfz
CORS
4o
p
sf
TIMB.
Changez en La ♭ Mi ♭
arco
p expressif
arco
p expressif
Unis
arco
p expressif
p

106
9
1re et 2e FL.
molto cresc.
HAUTB.
molto cresc.
COR ANG.
molto cresc.
CL.
molto cresc.
molto cresc.
sfz
Bons
molto cresc.
sfz
molto cresc.
sfz
CORS
molto cresc.
sf
9
arco
molto cresc. très expressif
Div.
f
molto cresc.
Div.
f
molto cresc.
Div.
f
molto cresc.
f
Unis
molto cresc.

111
1re et 2e FL.
HAUTB.
COR ANG.
CL.
1er et 2e Bons.
à 2
cuivrez
CORS
f
ff

116
10
Modéré mais toujours très rythmé
pp
TROMP. (Sourdines)
pp
1re HARPE
ppp
2e HARPE ppp
TIMB.
ppp
10
Modéré mais toujours très rythmé
pizz.
pp
Velle
Div.
pizz.
pp
Div.
pizz.
ppp

125
TROMP.
1re HARPE
2e HARPE
TIMB.
Div.

132
un peu rapproché
TROMP.
1re HARPE
2e HARPE
TIMB.

139
11
1re et 2e FL.
pte FL.
HAUTB.
COR ANG.
CL.
1er et 2e Bons
TROMP.
(Otez les Sourdines)
1re HARPE
2e HARPE
TIMB.
p
peu
a
peu
cresc.
pizz.
Div.
Unis

145
1re et 2e FL.
12
pte FL.
HAUTB.
COR ANG.
CL.
Bons
CORS
f
TIMB.
12
Unis

152
1re et 2e FL.
pte FL.
HAUTB.
COR ANG.
CL.
à 2
Bons
CORS
1°
3°
cresc.
TROMP.
f vibrant sans dureté
1er et 2e TROMB.
3e TROMB. et TUBA
2 HARPES
TIMB.
CYMB.
TAMB. M.
mf molto cresc.
13
arco
molto cresc.
Unis
Div.

158
1re et 2e FL.
HAUTB.
CL.
1er et 2e Bons
CORS
TROMP.
1er et 2e TROMB.
3e TROMB. et TUBA
2 HARPES
TIMB.
CYMB.
TAMB. M.

162
1re et 2e FL.
HAUTB.
CL.
1er et 2e Bons
CORS
TROMP.
1er et 2e TROMB.
3e TROMB. et TUBA
2 HARPES
TIMB.
CYMB.
TAMB. M.

166

1re et 2e Fl.
HAUTB.
COR ANG.
CL.
à 2
1er et 2e Bons
CORS
TROMP.
1er et 2e TROMB.
3e TROMB. et TUBA
2 HARPES
TIMB.
CYMB.
TAMB. M.
Unis

170

1re et 2e FL.

HAUTB.

ff

COR ANG.

CL.

à 2

ff

Bons

ff

ff très soutenu

CORS

ff très soutenu

ff très soutenu

TROMP.

1er et 2e ff très soutenu

TROMB.

ff très soutenu

3e TROMB. et TUBA

ff très soutenu

TIMB.

ff

3

3

CYMB.

ff

ff

TAMB. M.

ff

ff

ff

ff

ff

174
14
I° tempo
1re et 2e FL.
à 2
pp
HAUTB.
pp
2°
COR ANG.
pp
CL.
pp
Bons
CORS
TROMP.
1er et 2e TROMB.
3e TROMB. et TUBA
TIMB.
TAMB. M.
14
I° tempo
Div.
pp
pp
Div.
pp

180
1re et 2e FL.
p
pp
pte FL.
pp
HAUTB.
p
à 2
pp
COR ANG.
p
pp
CL.
p
pp
1er et 2e Bons
pp

186
15
1re et 2e FL.
cre
scen
do
f
pte FL.
HAUTB.
COR ANG.
CL.
Bons
1er et 2e CORS
f expressif et très soutenu
Div.

192
De plus en plus sonore et en serrant le mouvement
HAUTB.
più f
COR ANG.
più f
CL.
più f
più f
Bons
più f
più f
CORS
3o
f
De plus en plus sonore et en serrant le mouvement
più f
più f
più f
più f
più f

198
1re et 2e FL.
16
fff
pte FL.
fff
HAUTB.
fff
COR ANG.
ff
CL.
ff
Bons
ff
CORS
ff
ff
TROMP.
ff
ff
1er et 2e TROMB.
ff
3e TROMB. et TUBA
ff
16
fff
ff
fff
ff
fff
fff
fff

204
1re et 2e FL.
Même mouvt
COR ANG.
pp
CL.
pp
pp
BONS
pp
1o
pp
CORS
3o
pp
TROMP.
CYMB.
tr
ff
dim. molto
(baguette de Timb.)
pp
TAMB.M.
pp
Même mouvt
Div.
dim. molto
pp
dim. molto
pizz.
pp
pizz.
pp

209
17
à 2
FL.
HAUTB.
COR ANG.
CL.
Bons
CORS
2º
4º
HARPE
TIMB.
CYMB.
TAMB. M.
pp
Unis

213
Fl.
Hautb.
Cor ang.
Cl.
Bons
Cors
1°
3°
Harpe
Timb.
Cymb.
Tamb m.
pp
f

216
18
à 2
Fl.
Hautb.
Cor ang.
Cl.
Bons
Cors
Tromb.
Harpe
Timb.
Cymb.
Tamb. M.
Unis
18

221
1re et 2e FL.
HAUTB.
COR ANG.
CL.
Bons - scen - - do
- scen - - do
à 2
CORS
- scen - do
TROMB.
- - scen - - - do
- - scen - - - do
- - scen - - - do
- - scen - - - do

225
8
FL.
HAUTB.
COR ANG.
CL.
à 2
BONS
ff
CORS
TROMB.
f
ff

229
19
FL.
HAUTB.
COR ANG.
CL.
BONS
1o
p
CORS
TROMB.
19
dim.
dim.

233
più p
Bous
pp
2
p
CORS
3°
2
p
1er et 2e TROMB.
pp
3e TROMB. et TUBA
pp
CYMB.
pp
TAMB. M.
p
Div.
pp
pp
pizz.
sf
sf
p dim.
p dim.

237
1re 2e et 3e FL.
p dim.
HAUTB.
1o
p
p
p
1o
p
Bons
pp
CORS
TROMP.
p dim.
pp
p dim.
pp
1er et 2e TROMB.
pp
3e TROMB. et TUBA
pp
CYMB.
pp
pizz.
pp
pizz.
pp
arco
pp léger
pizz.
pp
arco
pp léger

241
20
più p
Bons
pp
(Sourdines)
TROMP.
TROMB.
CYMB.
TAMB. M.
20
pp

245
1re 2e et 3e FL.
pp dim.
HAUTB.
1o
p
p
p
1o
pp
Bons
pp
ppp
TROMP.
ppp
1er et 2e TROMB.
pp
3e TROMB. et TUBA
pp
CYMB.
pp
pp
pp

249
1er et 2e FL.
Un peu retenu
doux et expressif
HAUTB.
doux et expressif
1er Bon
TUBA
Div.
pizz. pp
pizz. pp
pizz. pp
velles et C.B.
Sourdines
255
1er et 2e FL.
21
HAUTB.
COR ANG.
dim.
più p
CL.
dim.
più p
1er Bon
più p
Sourdines cuivrez
CORS
Sourdines cuivrez
TUBA
1re HARPE
più pp
più pp
più pp

263
1e et 2e FL.
a tempo
pp
HAUTB.
pp
COR ANG.
CL.
pp
Bons
pp
2o
pp
ppp
Cuivrez
Cuivrez
CORS
pp
ppp
Cuivrez
Cuivrez
TAMB. M.
ppp
a tempo
ppp
ppp
ppp
pp et toujours en s'éloignant davantage
du bout de l'archet
pp
du bout de l'archet
pp
pp et toujours en s'éloignant davantage

269
22
Sourdines
1°
p
CORS
Sourdines
3°
p
1re TROMP.
Sourdines
p
più p

274
TIMB.
ppp
ppp
CYMB.
ppp
Div.
ppp
pizz.
ppp
Div.
ppp
pizz.
ppp

III. Sirènes

[Sirens]

3

1re FL.
pp
CL.
CORS
pp
p
1re HARPE
2e HARPE
MEZZO-SOP.
p
pp
Div.
ppp
Div.
Div.
pizz.
p

5

7
FL.
HAUTB.
CL.
CORS
1re HARPE
2e HARPE
SOPRANI
arco
pizz.

10
FL.
pp
COR ANG.
p expressif un peu en dehors
Bons
CORS
p
p
1re HARPE pp
2e HARPE pp
pp
pp
pp
pp
Vlles Div
pp

13
FL.
1re et 2e
HAUTB.
COR ANG.
CL.
Bons
expressif
CORS
1re HARPE
2e HARPE
SOPRANI
MEZZO-SOP.
Div. en 6
pp sur la touche
Div.
pizz.
sur la touche
Div.
ôtez les sourdines aux 2ds pupitres
ôtez les sourdines aux 2ds pupitres
ôtez les sourdines aux 2ds pupitres

18

FL.

HAUTB.

à 2

COR ANG.

CL.

1o

à 2

Bons

à 2

CORS

1re HARPE

2e HARPE

SOP.

M-SOP.

pp sur la touche

Position nat.

pp sur la touche

Position nat.

pp sur la touche

pp sur la touche

pp sur la touche

Div.

pizz.

22

2
FL.
p
p
pp
HAUTB.
à 2
p
pp
COR ANGL.
p
più p
pp
CL.
à 2
p
pp
1er et 2e Bons
1er et 2e CORS
p
dim
pp
MEZZO-SOP.
p
pp
2
ôtez les sourdines aux 1ers pupitres
ôtez les sourdines aux 1ers pupitres
ôtez les sourdines aux 2ds pupitres
p e dim molto
p e dim molto
Unis
Div.
p e dim molto
* seulement les 2ds pupitres avec sourdine
* id. id. id. id.
Les 1ers enlevent la sourdine
più p

26
FL.
pp
pp
CORS
pp
p très expressif
SOP.
MEZZO-SOP.
pp très léger
pp très léger
pp très léger
pp très léger
pp très léger
pizz.
pp très léger

28
FL.
pp
HAUTB.
COR ANGL.
CL.
Bons
CORS
TROMP.
SOPRANI
MEZZO-SOP.
à 2
1. 2.
p très expressif
pizz.

31
FL.
HAUTB.
COR ANG.
CL.
Bons
TROMP.
MEZZO-SOP.
p

33

36
FL.
à 2
HAUTB.
1°
COR ANG.
CL.
Bons
à 2
COR
3e
1re HARPE
2e HARPE
SOP
M-SOP
pizz.
pizz.
pizz.
pizz.
pizz.
pizz.

40
4
FL.
HAUTB.
COR ANG.
CL
à 2
Bons
CORS
accrochez mi ♭, do ♭, la ♭, fa ♮ ré ♯, si ♮, sol ♯, mi ♯
1re HARPE
en remontant fa ♮, la ♭, do ♭, ré ♭ mi ♯, sol ♯, si ♮, do ♯
2e HARPE
M-SOP.
à 8 p très expressif et très soutenu
arco
1rs Vons
Div.
avec la pointe de l'archet
2ds Vons
ALT.
Vlles
pp avec la pointe de l'archet

43
FL.
HAUTB.
COR ANG.
CL.
Bons
CORS
2e HARPE
M-SOP.
1rs Vons
2ds Vons
ALT.
Vlles

46
FL.
à 2
HAUTB.
COR ANG.
CL.
Bons
Sourdines
CORS
Sourdines
1re HARPE
glissando
2e HARPE
Lab Réb
SOP
M-SOP.
pizz
arco
pizz
arco
pizz
arco

50
5
FL.
HAUTB.
COR ANG.
CL.
Bons
CORS
1re HARPE
2e HARPE
SOP.
M-SLP.
retenu
f
dim.
p
pp
dim
Div.

55

CL.

Un peu plus lent

pp

B^ons

CORS

1º

pp sourdine

3º

pp sourdine

1re HARPE

2^e HARPE

SOP.

1. 2.

p doux et soutenu

3. 4.

p

M-SOP.

pp

Un peu plus lent

pp

pp

Div.

pp

60
FL.
CL.
CORS
SOPRANI
Div.
Div.
pp
p

65
FL.
CL.
CORS
4 SOPRANI
p
pp
pp
pp
p
pp
pp
pp
pp
pp
pp
pp
pp

69
6 En animant surtout dans l'expression
Fl.
Hautb.
à 2
p
Cl.
2°
p
Bons
p
Cors
pp
pp
pp
Sopr'ni
6 En animant surtout dans l'expression
pp
p très expressif
p très expressif
p très expressif
p
p

73
FL.
HAUTB.
COR ANG.
CL.
à 2
Bons
CORS
SOPRANI
mf très expressif
mf très expressif

77
7 Serrez
FL.
HAUTB. à 2
COR ANG.
CL.
Bons
1er
CORS
3e
7 Serrez
à 2
Unis

81
Retenu avec force
FL.
HAUTB.
COR ANG.
CL.
BONS
CORS
TROMP.
Retenu avec force
Div.
dim
p
mf
f
ff

85
8
Tempo un peu plus lent
HAUTB.
pp
COR ANGL.
p
CL.
p
Bons
2°
p
1°
CORS
3°
TROMP. (1°)
très dim.
p expressif et soutenu
SOPRANI
8
Tempo un peu plus lent
p
più p
pp
dim
pizz.

89
1re FL.
à 2
HAUTB.
COR ANG.
CL.
Bons
2º
CORS
1º
3º
SOPRANI
expressif et soutenu
sur la touche
tr
sur la touche
tr
pizz.
arco
pizz.
arco

93
1re FL.
HAUTB.
COR ANG.
CL.
Bons
CORS
1º
3º
à 2
SOPRANI
sur la touche
sur la touche
arco
arco

97
1re FL.
à 2
HAUTB.
COR ANG.
CL.
Bons
2º
CORS
Sourdine
SOPRANI
Div.
Unis.

101
9
Revenir progressivement au 1º Tempo
FL.
3º
COR ANG.
CL.
1º
1er et 2e Bons
1º Solo
cuivrez
CORS
HARPE
SOPRANI
8 MEZZO-SOP.
à bouche fermée
à bouche fermée
9
Revenir progressivement au 1º Tempo
Div.
pizz.
pizz.
pizz.
velles

104
En augmentant peu à peu
FL.
HAUTB
1°
COR ANG.
CL.
pp
1er et 2e Bons
CORS
HARPE
8 2ds SOP.
En augmentant peu à peu
p
p

107
2º
FL.
HAUTB.
COR ANG.
CL.
1er et 2e Bons
1º sourdine
CORS
3º sourdine
4º cuivrez bouché
8 1res SOP.
a 4
Div.
8 2des SOP.
3
6
p
velles

109
FL.
HAUTB.
COR ANG.
CL.
1er et 2e Bons
CORS
8 1rs SOP.
à 4
8 2ds SOP.
ALTOS
Velles

111

10
1º Tempo
1re FL.
HAUTB.
pp
2º
CL.
1er et 2e Bons
CORS
1º
3º
3 TROMP.
doux et expressif
les 2e et 3e avec sourdines
1re HARPE
mf
2e HARPE
8 1rs SOP.
mf expressif et soutenu
8 2ds SOP.
sfz > pp

114
HAUTB.
2º
COR ANG.
CL.
1er et 2e Bons
p
pp
1º
p cuivrez — sans dureté
2º
CORS
3º
p cuivrez — sans dureté
4º
3 TROMP.
1re HARPE mf
2e HARPE mf
8 1res SOP.
8 2ds SOP.
sur la touche
sur la touche
sur la touche
sur la touche
sur la touche
sur la touche
sur la touche
sur la touche

117
FL.
CLAR.
1er et 2e Bons
CORS
ôtez les sourdines
ôtez les sourdines
3 TROMP.
1re HARPE
2e HARPE
8 1res SOP.
8 2ds SOP.
Unis.

120
1.er et 2.e B.ons
CORS
à 4
8 1.res SOP.
8 2.ds SOP.
doux et expressif.
mettez les sourdines
mettez les sourdines
mettez les sourdines
mettez les sourdines
Div.
mettez les sourdines
Unis.
Unis.
pizz.

124
11
CLAR.
1er et 2d Bons
8 1es SOP.
8 2ds SOP.
piu p
più p
11
pp
pizz.
mettez les sourdines
Div.
velles

128
Retenir
Plus lent et en retenant jusqu'à la fin
1re FL.
HAUTB.
CL.
1er et 2e Bons
CORS
2e
3e
1re HARPE
2e HARPE
4 SOP.
4 M-SOP.
pp
p
Retenir
Plus lent et en retenant jusqu'à la fin
Unis.
Velles
Div.
arco

132
12
1re FL.
pp
ppp
HAUTB.
COR ANG.
doux et expressif
p
p
pp
CL.
pp
ppp
1º
CORS
pp
ppp
1re HARPE
pp
2e HARPE
pp
8 MEZZO-SOP.
bouche fermée
bouche fermée
12
più pp
ppp
pppp
les 1ers pupitres seulement

137

1re FL.
ppp
HAUTB.
pp
TROMP.
doux et expressif.
p
très dim.
1re HARPE
pp
8 MEZZO-SOP.
pp
pp
pp
pp
pp
pp
sur la touche
ppp
sur la touche
ppp
sur la touche
ppp
position naturelle
pp

END OF EDITION